Paper
Space
Craft

Carmel D. Morris

First published by Omnibus Books, 1992
Reprinted several times by Scholastic Sydney and New York
This edition Copyright 2012, Big One Productions
ISBN-10: 1466406089
ISBN-13 978-1466406087
Cover design: Big One Productions
Typeset in Palatino Linotype 11pt
This edition is printed in the United States of America

10 9 8 7 6 5 4 3 2

Preface

Hi, I'm Dwight from Big 1 Productions. This book is written by a best-selling author of over 35 books including *Advanced Paper Aircraft Volumes 1, 2 and 3* (Harper Collins), *Fold Your Own Jumbo Aircraft* (Harper/Angus & Robertson), and *The Best Paper Aircraft*, (Putnam).

If you like science fiction or science fact for that matter, and especially if spacecraft fascinates you, then this book is for you. All the models have been tested and glide well through an atmosphere such as Earth's, and so far no models have burned up on re-entry!

One day Richard Branson will test these models and in space, your spacecraft will go on and on.

Inspired by Battlestar Galactica, Star Wars and other classics, along with real-world examples, this book will test your Origami folding skills from really simple to advanced craft. More than just paper aircraft, you'll have a lot of fun folding these great space models at home, your school or university, or in the office.

Now get ready with your Letter or A4 sheets of paper and start folding, because the right stuff is in you to exceed your paper limitations. Happy flying, space cowboys 'n girls!

Dwight Edwards, Big 1 Productions

Contents

Introduction

Greetings Earth dudes! You are now entering a galaxy of paper rockets, UFOs and planetary defense craft. Some of the models are designed to inspire discovery and inventiveness, while others reflect the universe of space conquest.

Space... The Final Frontier...

The idea of extra-terrestrial life has fascinated human beings for centuries. We are a race of beings on one planet among billions of stars and planets in our galaxy alone. There are billions of other galaxies out there and probability tells us that somewhere there must be other life forms.

Time is an expanse, just as space is, and this means that not all planets exist in the same time period. It could take thousands of years traveling at the speed of light before we discover if there are other life forms. Our own world could be gone by then! However we constantly hear of UFO sightings. Are aliens or even members of our own species visiting us from the future?

Will we even know? Does it really concern avid folders of paper aircraft, or spacecraft? Why the hell am I talking about all this here?

Because out there inspires all of us. To be out there one day is a dream that may one day come true.

Our knowledge is limited but our imagination is infinite. Building your paper spaceships could be the start to building real-life space stations in the near future!

All the models in this book are clearly explained in step-by-step diagrams that accompany instructional text as you progress. For a diagram, instructional text appears *before* the related diagram. Most of the models are crease-folded first to establish symmetry. The crease-fold is indicated with the thin central line shown in the 'Step 1' diagram for most models.

If you are using an e-book reader, don't forget to use the 'zoom' function where available, if you need to see the images closely.

This book also has tips on throwing, so if you're going to be space-bound, put on your space suit first!

About the paper sizes

All models in this book are made from standard A4 paper, which also works well for US letter. Measurements are in most cases provided in centimeters (1cm = .39 or 2/5 of an inch).

Paper thickness (weight) should be in the range of 80 to 100 GSM (Grams per Square Meter). This level of density ensures good rigidity in folds, i.e. better creases. Do not use paper that is thicker, since more complicated folds can come undone.

Enjoy!

Have fun, fold well and remember; in space no one can hear you fold your spacecraft.

Folding Symbols

Models in this book use the following symbols.

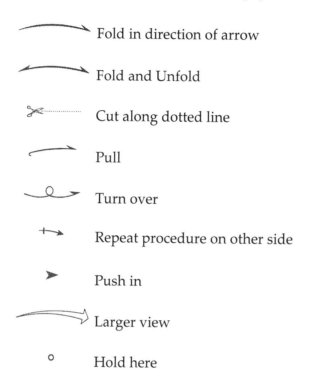

Fold in direction of arrow

Fold and Unfold

Cut along dotted line

Pull

Turn over

Repeat procedure on other side

Push in

Larger view

Hold here

Folding Techniques

If you are lousy at Origami, or just need a little practice, find some small pieces of paper to get your folding practice to perfection, and follow the directions shown below.

Valley Fold

This is indicated with a line of dashes.

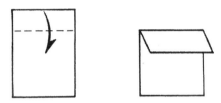

Crease Fold

Valley-folded over and then unfolded to make the thin solid crease line as shown in the right-hand image.

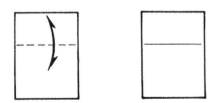

Mountain Fold

Folded behind and indicated by a line of dots and dashes.

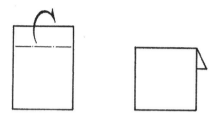

X-ray

X-ray or hidden view, indicated by a dotted line.

Push in

This is typically a double-mountain fold pushed into a paper model; quadruple folds occur for pushing in the pointed end of a model consisting of four sides.

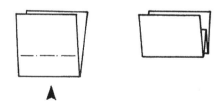

Rabbit Ear Fold

It is highly recommended that you practice folding 'rabbit ears' as this type of fold is common in Origami.

Grab a piece of A4 or Letter paper and try the following...

1. Fold top-left corner diagonally across to meet the right-hand side.

2. Unfold.

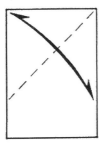 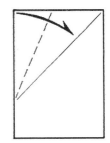

3. (Left image below) Fold the top-left corner again so that it meets the crease made from Step 1.

4. (Right-hand image) Unfold.

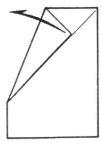 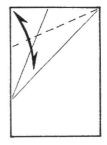

5. (Left image) Fold top-end down in the same manner as, but opposite to that in Step 3.

6. (Center image) Now pinch the top-left corner with your thumb and forefinger and fold the entire point down to meet the crease made from Step 1. Flatten the point.

7. (Right-hand image) Your rabbit ear is complete!

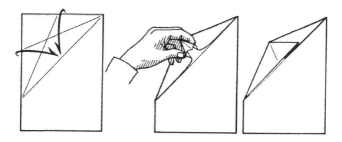

You are now armed with the skills to commence building your own paper spacecraft.

Simple Flying Saucer

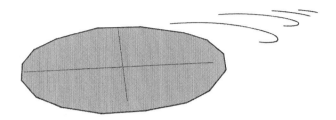

So simple my dog can probably make this one; he should, since he's slobbered over my other ones after catching them!

1. Use an A4 or Letter sheet and fold a diagonal to make a square.

2. Unfold and snip off the unused piece.

3. You now have a square. Neat.

4. (Left image) Fold an opposite diagonal to the one you made in Step 1.

5. (Right image) The two diagonal crease folds intersect at the center. Fold all corners in to meet this center point.

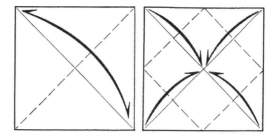

6. Unfold the corners.

7. Fold the corners in to meet the crease folds made in step 5.

8. Fold the new edges in again to meet the same crease folds made in step 5.

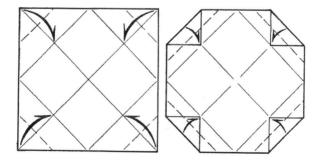

9. (Left image) Fold in the open-ended sides.

10. (Right image) Fold in the other corners as shown in the enlarged view to 'round out' the craft.

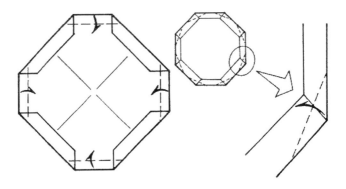

11. The finished craft! Paint it in luminous colors so it glows as you throw it. Spook your neighbors at Halloween.

"Klaatu barada nikto!"

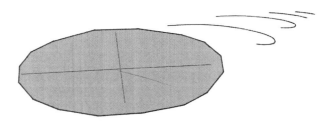

U-Wing Early Warp Drive Craft

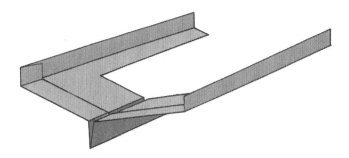

Looks almost like an early Warp drive USS star class ship that Zefram Cochrane would be proud of! This simple craft can perform some great stunts when thrown hard and high against a moderate solar wind.

1. Start with a sheet of A4 already folded in half and unfolded as shown. Fold the top end down over and over again, five times at around 18mm intervals (or 3/4 of an inch).

2. Fold in half.

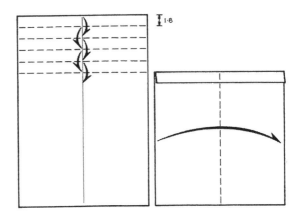

3. (Upper image) Mark out the measurements as shown with a pencil, and then cut along the dotted line, cutting both sides of the paper simultaneously.

4. (Lower image) Measure 2.2cm from the top edge and fold the edge behind. Repeat on the other side. Make the fuselage section by folding the wings down by 1.5cm.

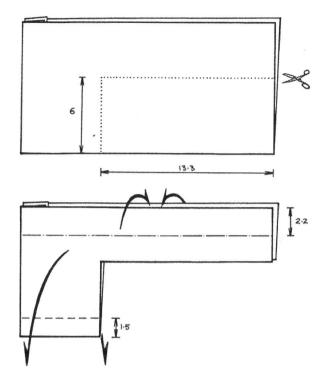

5. The completed craft, ready to challenge the laws of physics! "Aye Cap'n!"

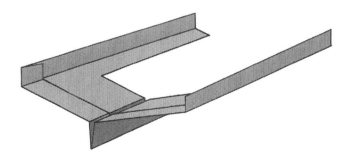

Rocket Glider

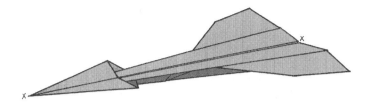

Is it a rocket or a glider? Both! After reaching maximum altitude, it will glide safely towards Earth for final touchdown; no burning up in the atmosphere for this craft!

1. (Top image) Use strong (100gsm) A4 paper, crease-folded as shown. Fold the corners in as for a standard paper dart.

2. (Middle image) Turn the paper over.

3. (Lower image) Fold leading edges in towards the center-crease, at the same time flicking out the flaps underneath (these are shown on the diagram as a hidden fold).

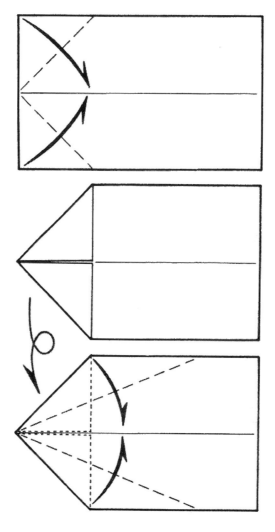

4. (Top image) Fold sides in as shown. The edges actually go under the upper flaps.

5. (Middle image) Should now look more streamlined. Turn the model over.

6. (Lower image) Fold forward section sides in to meet at the center.

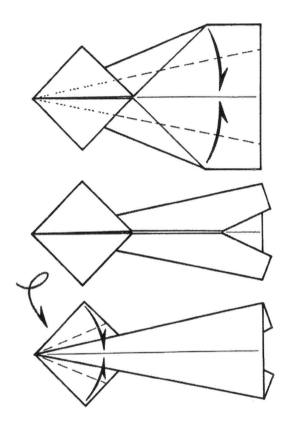

7. (Top image) Should look like this; now turn the model over.

8. (Middle image) Fold wing flaps outwards, the creases meeting at the center crease.

9. (Lower image) Fold in half behind.

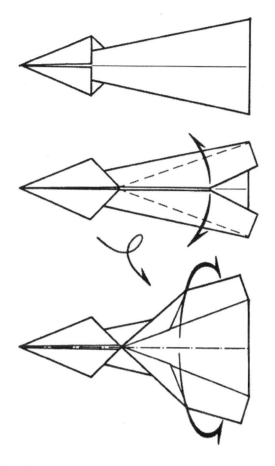

10. Seal the fuselage with sticky tape and then fold the wings down in the approximate position shown.

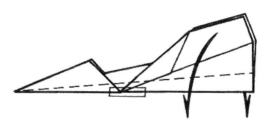

11. Completed. You may need to seal the two flaps to the fuselage with tape. For a high-speed rocket, seal the entire fuselage with tape from one end to the other (x-x).

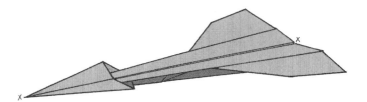

UF 0

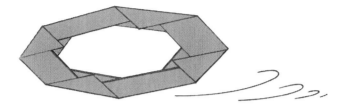

This is a lightweight yet strong craft that uses eight segments to ensure rigidity for good Frisbee throwing. It'll fly past so fast folks won't be able to identify it!

1. (Upper left image) Get eight pieces of A4 or Letter paper and make them square (or find some nice colored square Origami paper). Starting with the first piece, mountain-fold the square in half and then unfold.

2. (Upper right image) Fold and unfold the two diagonals.

3. (Lower image) Bring the sides together; bringing the top ends down towards the bottom.

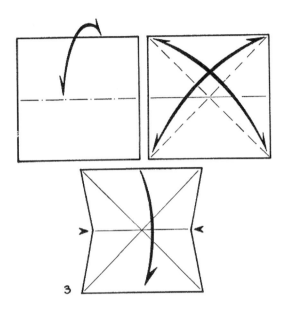

4. (Upper image) You're almost there. Flatten the fold.

5. (Lower image) Fold the top point down to meet the bottom edge. Now repeat Steps 1 to 5 for the remaining seven pieces of square paper.

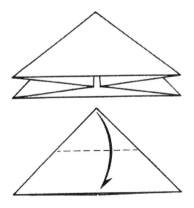

6. (Upper image) Having folded eight pieces, slot them together. Place piece A facing you as shown. Turn piece B upside down (noting the hidden point underneath). Slot the left point of B under the flap of A. Tape them together. Repeat the procedure until all eight sections are secured; forming the ring-shaped UFO.

7. (Lower image) Almost there!

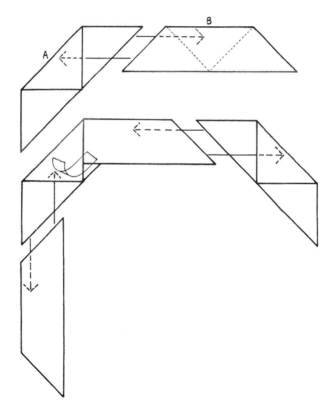

8. Complete UFO. Hold as you would for a normal Frisbee and fling horizontally at the nearest

primitive planet, such as your neighbor's back yard.

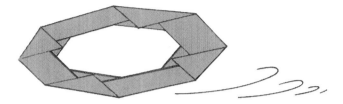

CFO (Crazy Flying Object)

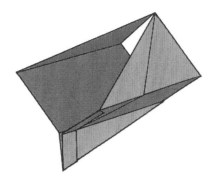

Watching something like this on your radar screen would drive you crazy; causing you to believe some alien is showing off his flying skills. This craft flies erratically; no one would blame you for throwing this in the classroom since the trajectory could have originated from anyone!

1. (Top image) Begin with a sheet of paper crease-folded in half. Fold top right and left corners in to meet the center crease. The creases of these folds must finish at the bottom right and left corners respectively.

2. (Middle image) Fold the top end down by 1cm, five times.

3. (Lower image) Fold in half behind.

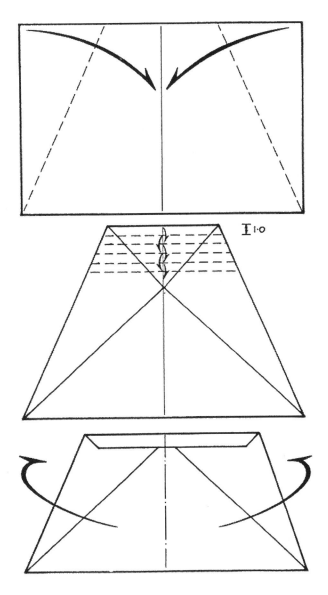

4. (Upper image) Mountain and valley fold the wings on both sides.

5. (Lower image) Seal the fuselage with tape at the front. Bring the two outer wing tips together and carefully join them with tape.

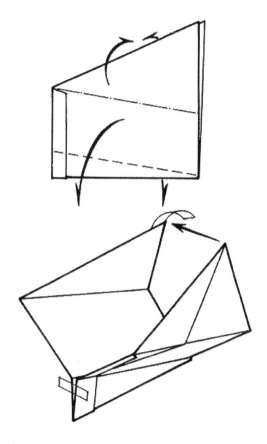

6. Complete and ready to drive someone nuts!

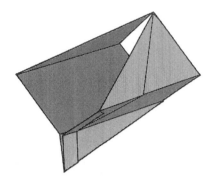

Two-In-One Rocket

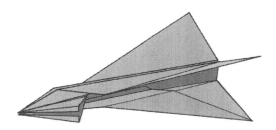

When thrown, this craft will divide into two jets; or you could seal the rocket permanently or keep two gliders, the choice is yours. Why not make two and have both versions?

1. (Top left image) Begin with a sheet of crease-folded A4 or Letter paper. Mark out the 14cm down and then fold the corner from the top center crease to the place you marked.

2. (Top right image) Fold entire side from top center to bottom right corner.

3. (Lower left image) Fold the small point back to the right along the fold made from Step 2.

4. (Lower right image) Repeat Steps 1 to 3 for the left side. Now fold the model behind in half.

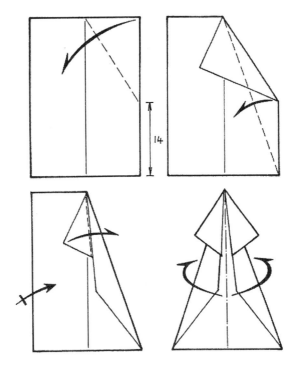

5. (Upper image) Have the model facing you horizontally. Fold the front points down on both sides.

6. (Lower image) Fold down the wings in the approximate positions shown here. The fold should be parallel to the bottom edge.

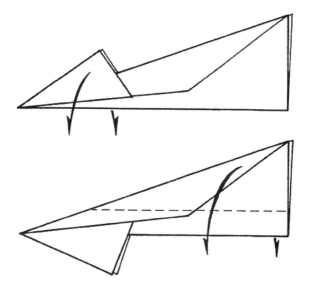

7. (Upper image) Fold the front points back up along the new creases. Fold the tail wings up from the bottom edge to the right-hand point.

8. (Lower image) Fold front fins down in approximate positions shown on both sides.

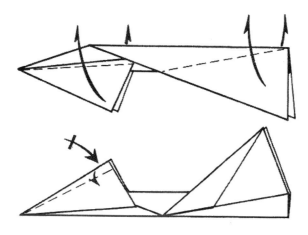

9. You have just finished one jet. Fold another jet following the previous instructions.

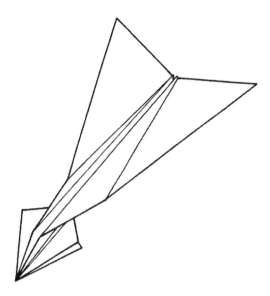

10. Using paperclips, join the two jets together along the bottom fold of their fuselages; one paperclip at each end. For a permanent rocket, join the two together with a strip of tape on each side along the base of the fuselages.

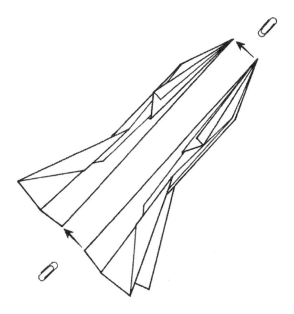

11. Complete and ready to separate high above in orbit! Make sure two jets are joined loosely for separation after during flight.

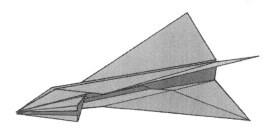

Lunar Lander

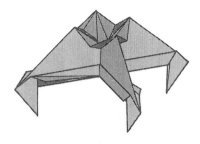

Have you ever considered humans as aliens on another world? One day you say? Well it actually happened in 1969 when we landed on the Moon! And our exploratory craft have landed on Venus and Mars and other exotic places. Now it's your turn to land your craft on a new strange alien frontier, but make sure it's not your kitty's litter tray!

1. Make a square from Letter or A4 paper, or get some of that gold Origami paper for that added reality (chocolate wrapper may also work). Make all creases as shown and bring the folds together.

2. Should look like this (see Steps 1-3 of the UFO for more details on folding). Now fold up the entire bottom of the model by around 3cm or 1 inch.

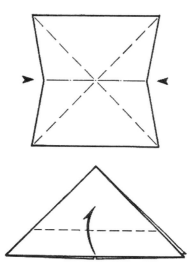

3. (Upper image) Unfold, turn model over and repeat the procedure outlined in Step 2 for the other side, reinforcing the crease just created. Make sure it is crisp and strong.

4. (Lower image) Now unfold the entire model. With the inside facing you, fold back all the edges along the creases created in Step 2.

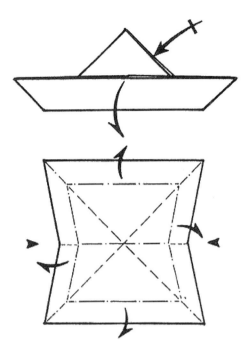

5. (Upper image) Bring the opposite sides together again to recreate the shape shown in Step 2, this time with upturned edges (the image is shown upside down).

6. (Lower image) Crease-fold each corner as shown. Then, turn each corner down and inside out.

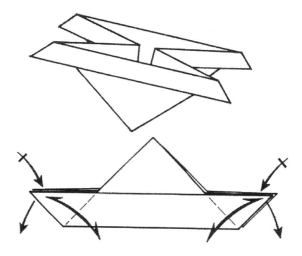

7. Should now look like this.

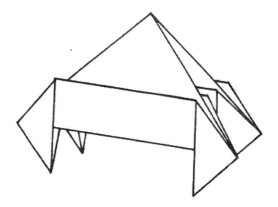

8. (Upper image) Fold entire model down the middle as shown, and then unfold it again. Repeat for the opposite side to strengthen the crease.

9. (Lower image) Fold bottom flap down so that it meets the bottom edge. Repeat on all other sides. Cut about 2cm off the top point. This measurement

41

will vary depending on how well you have folded the model up to this point.

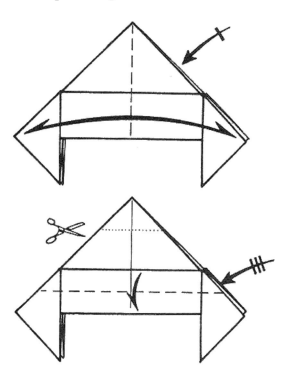

10. (Upper image) Fold up the lower left flap as shown, and repeat for each side, but only on the left of each side (A-B).

11. (Lower image) Open out the top like a flower by creasing and folding out all four sides as shown.

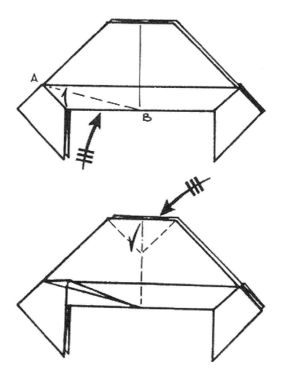

12. Complete and ready to land! Drop from a high place and watch it slowly rotate until it makes a soft landing. Hint: Do not let your model open out too wide (a wider distance between all landing feet) as it will be unstable in descent.

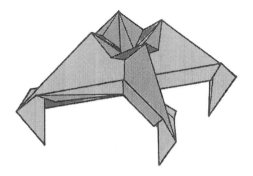

Simple H-Wing Cruiser

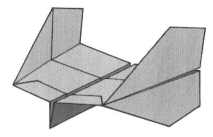

A variety of these things fly through many a sci-fi movie; now you can make your own! This one can do loops and arcs to dodge any Empirical craft, or annoy the cat!

1. With A4 paper creased vertically as shown, fold horizontally as shown.

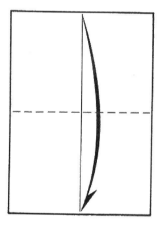

2. (Upper image) Fold top corners in to meet center crease, and then unfold.

3. (Lower image) Place finger under the top flap and fold the top half to the right.

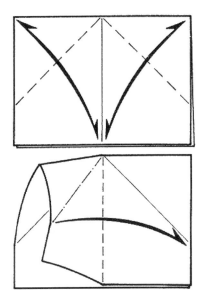

4. (Tope image) Turn the model over.

5. (Middle image) Repeat Step 3 for the other side.

6. (Lower image) Fold top nose down by 1.5cm, three times.

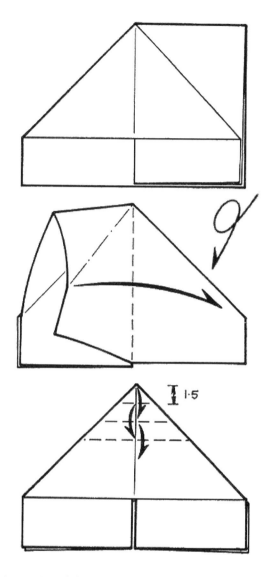

7. (Top image) Fold in wing fins at approximate angle shown. Do the same for the other side.

8. (Middle image) Fold model in half.

9. (Lower image) Fold wings down on both sides, 1cm above the bottom edge of the fuselage. Align the wing fins as shown in the finished model.

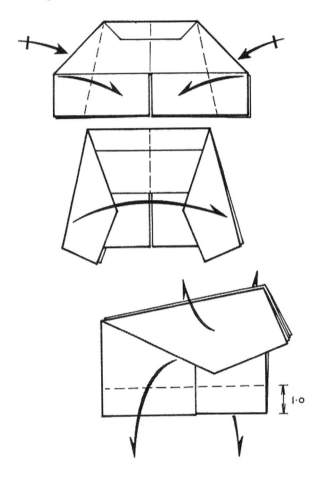

10. Complete! Throw hard and high. If you throw it hard at eye-level, it may dive bomb. If this happens, curl the trailing edge tail wing upwards.

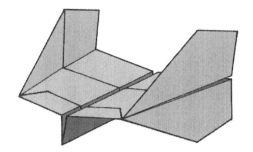

Bow Tie Fighter

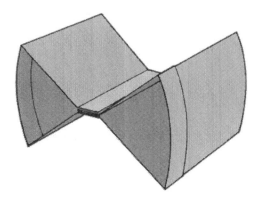

Bilateral Orbital Wing Twin Ion Engine

This craft has uncanny flying abilities, agile and suitable for the Empire – and it looks smart. Requires two sheets of A4 paper although one half can fly on its own! Or the model can split in two during flight for some amazing aerial stunts or attack vectors on two flanks!

1. (Upper image) Start with one sheet crease-folded in half lengthwise. Fold the top edge to meet the center crease and then unfold. This will establish a quarter-crease.

2. (Lower image) Fold over the top half of the paper by eighths, over and over again.

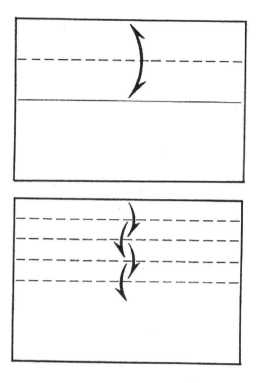

3. (Upper image) Should look like this. Mark out the center of the model and crease only the front (A). *Do not crease-fold the entire model in half!* Now fold the left end across to the right by one-third and then ford the right end to the left by one-third.

4. (Lower image, larger view) Fold edge on top flap to the right by 1.5cm. Now unfold the whole right side.

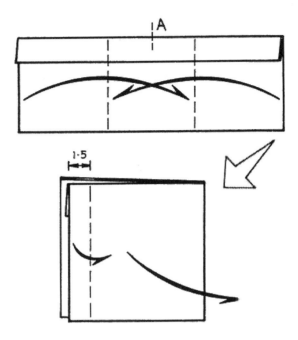

5. (Upper image) Fold opposite edge by 1.5cm to the left as shown. Now put this piece of paper aside and make another section, following Steps 1 to 5. *However*, this time at Step 3 have the piece turned over so that the flap created in Step 2 faces away from you. This will ensure a roll-and-tumble performance from your craft during flight.

6. (Lower images) Each piece can now fly on its own, either open or with its ends sealed with tape. Do not tape yet if you want both pieces joined.

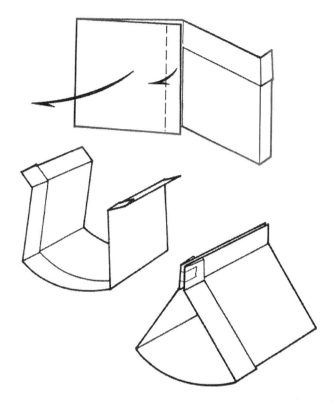

7. To join the two pieces, slot the edges together as shown. It is important that the outer curved sections of the model are not creased.

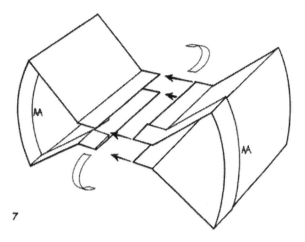

7

8. Tape the two sections you slotted together and the Bow Tie Fighter is complete. Curve up the middle tail edge for lift if necessary. *Note: Do not tape the two halves together if you want mid-air separation.*

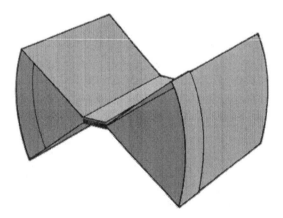

9. To throw, hold the center tail section with your finger and thumb. Throw forward horizontally; use force for stunts if the craft is sealed, otherwise

more gently for mid-flight separation if the craft is not sealed together.

Star Orbiter

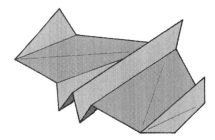

This is a slightly more complicated H-wing design that can glide gracefully when re-entering the atmosphere.

1. Start with Letter or A4 crease-folded down the middle. Fold and then unfold each top corner as shown.

2. (Middle image) Fold top corners down to meet the creases created in Step 1.

3. (Lower image) Make creases and bring in the folds.

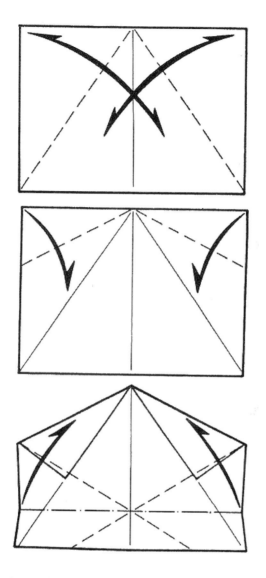

4. (Top image) Now flatten down the folds in directions shown.

5. (Middle image) Your model should look like this. Fold the end over by 1cm four times, and then fold the points of the flaps back and tuck them in as shown.

6. (Lower image) Fold model in half.

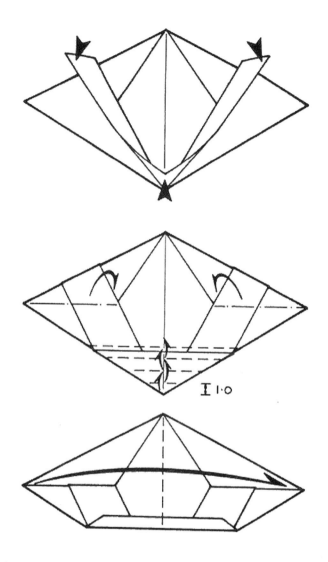

7. (Upper image) Crease the wing ends as shown.

8. (Lower image) Crease in half the flaps created in Step 7, then fold up the wings.

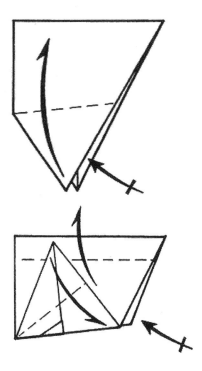

9. (Top two images) Open out the wing ends as shown in the closer detailed image at right, and press them flat to form vertical fins as shown in the lower image.

10. (Lower image) Crease wing at the angle indicated where it stems from the tail corner and repeat for the other wing.

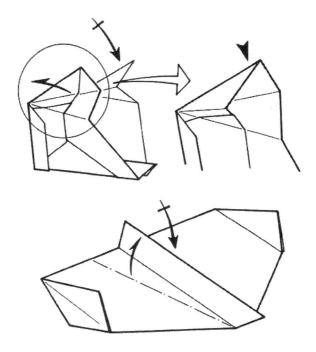

11. Complete and ready for orbit. This is an unorthodox craft; so a little practice is required to fly it well. Pinch the fuselage together and throw upwards at 30 degrees (too high and it will stall) with moderate force. Try sealing the fuselage together if you have problems. *Note: slide a paperclip on to the front of the fuselage if extra forward thrust is needed.*

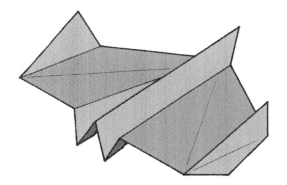

Cigar Shaped UFO

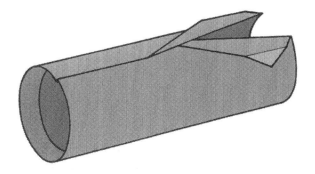

Many UFO sightings over the years described cigar-shaped craft hovering in the skies. Not zeppelins but stinking aliens! I wonder if such aliens smoke cigars. (I'll have to ask that one I met recently from Area 51 who seems to like cigarettes). Bad for your health, buddy.

To get this cigar to glide, I've cheated a bit by adding tail fins for stability. When I build a true anti-gravity device I'll let you know. :D

1. Place a sheet of un-creased paper before you. Measure out the first line 1.2cm from the top and then fold the paper over and over seven times.

2. Curl the paper; try not to leave creases anywhere.

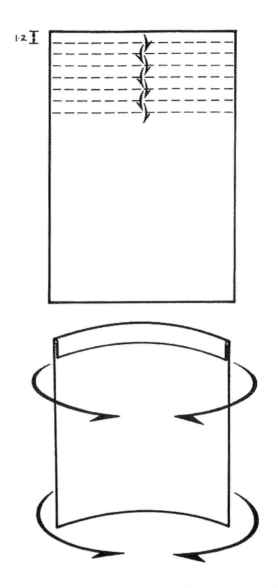

3. (Top image) Slot one end about 2cm into the other.
   Try to avoid creasing the craft as you do this.

4. (Middle image) Fold back the fins approximately at the angle shown.

5. (Lower image) Fold down the sides of each fin.

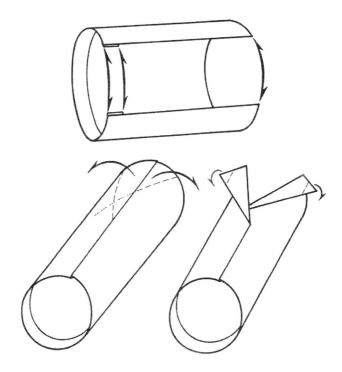

6. Complete and ready to scare the locals. Make sure they have their cameras out or you could video it gliding.

7. For throwing, curl your hand around the fuselage and try not to crease the craft. Aim the craft horizontally and throw with moderate force.

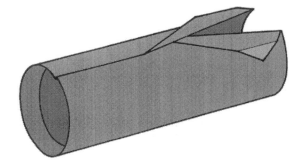

Cylon Warship

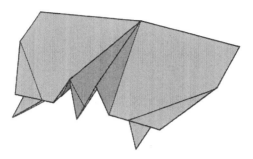

More true to the original Galactica series, this Cylon craft will spook anyone into submission.

I order you to make one now!

"By your command!"

1. Take a piece of A4 or Letter paper from one of your human victims and fold in the top corners to meet the center crease.

2. (Middle image) Make two rabbit-ear folds (creating a 'rabbit ear' is shown near the beginning of this book).

3. (Lower image) Fold the nose down.

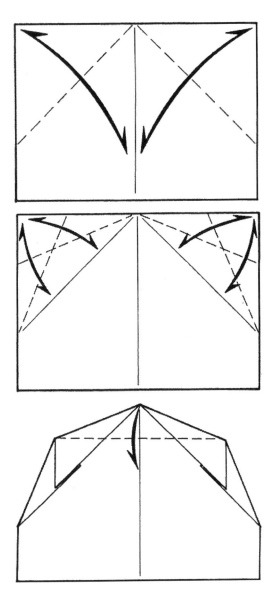

4. (Upper image) Fold the top leading edge behind, flipping forward the two 'guns'

5. (Lower image) Fold in half.

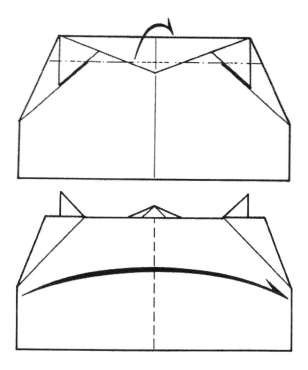

6. (Upper image) Fold the wings down in the approximate area shown.

7. (Lower image) Now fold the wings up so that the crease runs parallel along the base of the fuselage.

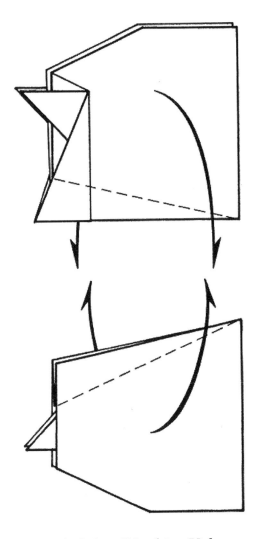

8. The completed Cylon Warship. Unless you are
   Baltar, this craft will not turn tail and run!

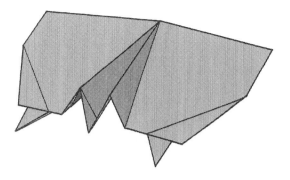

9. To throw, hold the rear end of your craft with finger and thumb. Gently drop your craft with a slight forward motion for it to glide smoothly. Try experimenting by sealing the fuselage and throwing with more force.

X-Wing Fighter

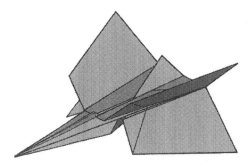

Levitate one of these effortlessly and you'll be a Jedi Knight in no time. This model flies true and is well balanced for throwing with more force; therefore to fly well, use the Force!

1. (Upper left image) Fold a vertically creased sheet of A4 horizontally in half behind and then unfold.

2. (Upper right image) Fold each top corner down to meet the one diagonally opposite and then unfold.

3. (Lower image) Fold top down while bringing in the sides (this step is very similar to Step 3 of UFO).

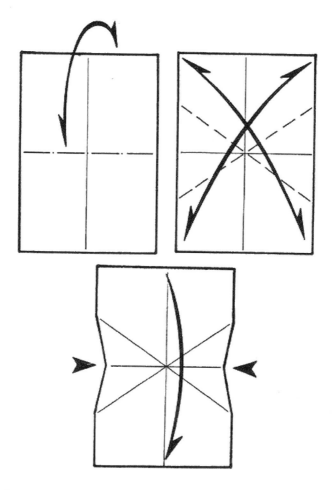

4. (Upper image) Now fold the left side along axis shown, and then the right side.

5. (Lower image) Fold the top flap up and to the right. Do the same for the flap underneath.

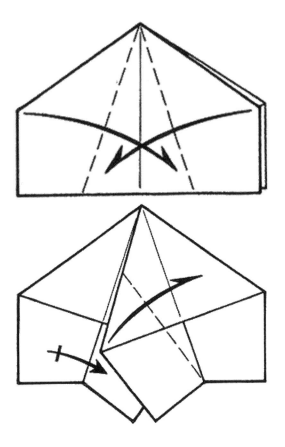

6. (Upper image) Complete Steps 4 and 5 for the other side.

7. (Lower image) Crease-fold the two flaps.

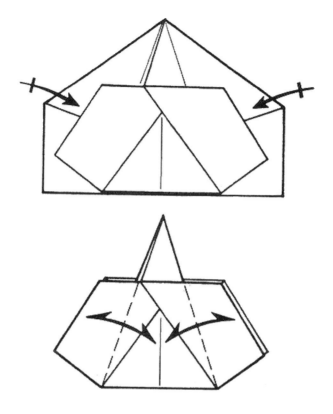

8. (Upper image) Fold the top layer to the right along the center crease. Do the same for the left-hand side.

9. (Lower image) Turn the model over.

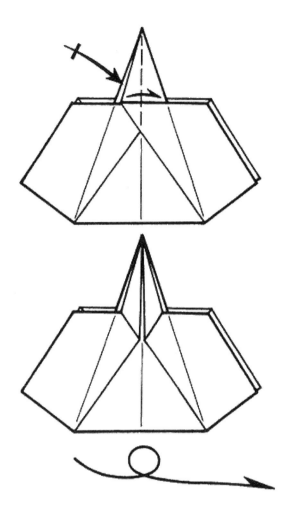

10. (Upper image) Note circled section; crease-fold only on this side.

11. (Lower image, closer view) Place your finger behind flap X and fold the entire section down and to the right. You're half way there with this fold.

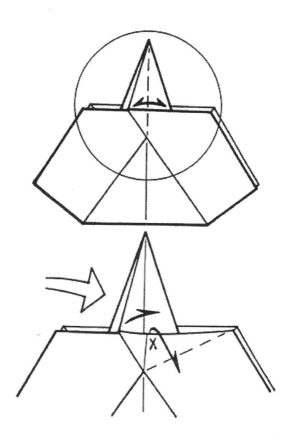

12. (Upper image) Repeat this procedure for the left side.

13. (Lower image) Crease-fold the wings on this side along the axis indicated, and then fold in half behind.

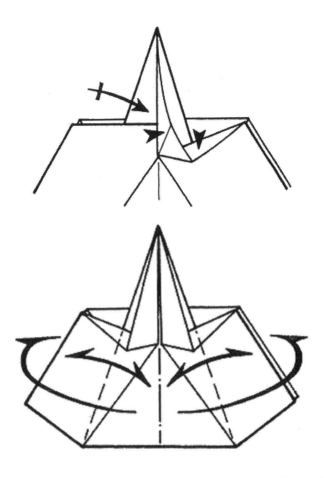

14. Push in the end of the fuselage to make the tail wing. Fold the main wings down. Adjust the wings so that they make a shallow X elevation shape.

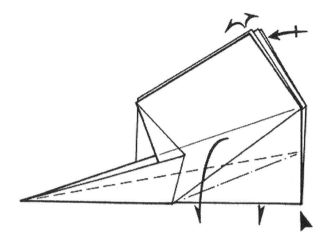

15. Completed X-wing. Simply aim and throw. This craft flies straight and true when folded correctly (and noting symmetry when folding). May the Force be with you!

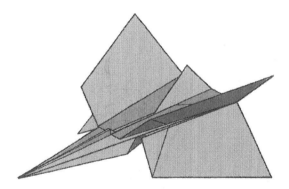

Star Blazer

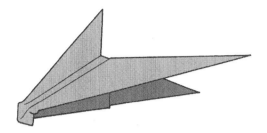

A zippy little craft that's easy to make. Looks a bit like a sparrow but probably seems alien to any bird on Earth!

1. With a piece of paper crease-folded, fold corners in.

2. Fold top point down to meet bottom edge.

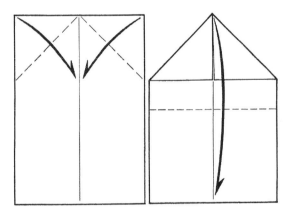

3. (Top image) Tuck your finger under 'O' and fold to the left, aligning edge A with center crease B.

4. (Middle image) Repeat for the left side.

5. (Lower image) Fold the sides in.

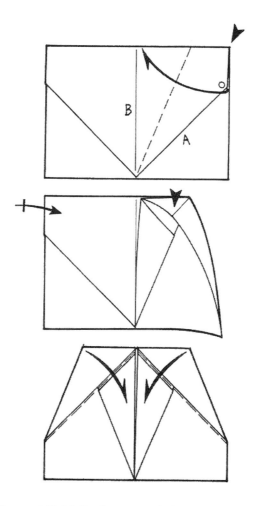

6. (Top image) Fold the lower point up.

7. (Middle image) Now secure the folds by folding the nose back by 1cm. Now fold the model in half behind.

8. (Lower image) Cut off the excess area to shape the wings along dotted lines indicated, and then fold new wing section.

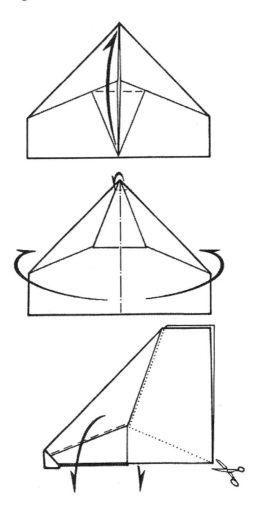

9. The completed craft. Throw fast and hard for best results. It actually flies better if the wings angle down slightly.

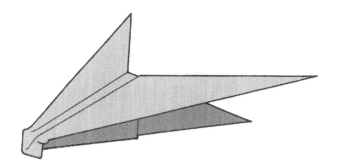

Millennium Falcon MKII

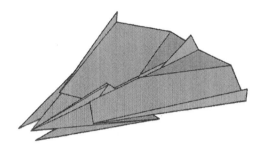

Not as unreliable as the first one, this craft will sleek through the skies and dodge any TIE fighters! This model glides nicely when folded using a sheet of A3 paper.

1. (Upper image) Start by following steps 1 to 5 for the X-Wing craft and then make the crease shown.

2. (Lower image) Open out the fold, reversing out the top crease so that it becomes a mountain fold instead of a valley fold, and then flatten it to the right.

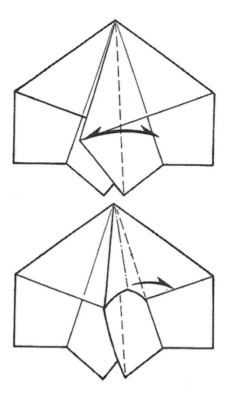

3. (Upper image) The craft should now look like this. Repeat Steps 1 and 2 on the other side.

4. (Lower image) Fold up the lower section.

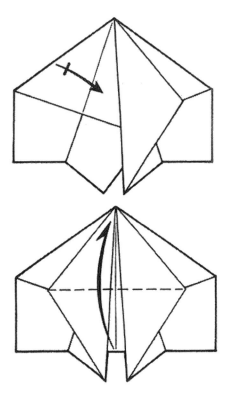

5. (Upper image) The craft should now look like this. Lift the edge marked A and fold it down to meet edge B, bringing the side points inwards. Flatten down.

6. (Lower image) This is what you should now have in front of you. Remember the points marked X and turn the model over.

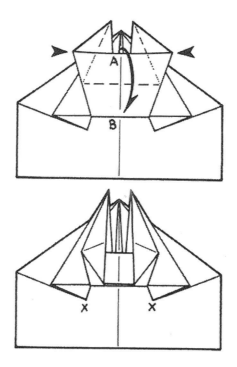

7. (Upper image) Noting the points marked X on the lower diagram for Step 6 (now underside); fold the right side to the left from point C along X (underneath).

8. (Lower image) Place your finger underneath and lift the edge indicated (from the arrow).

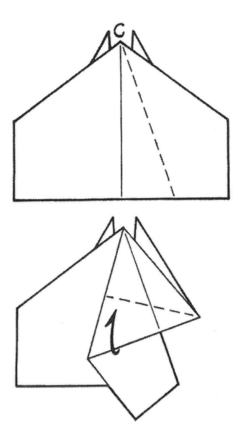

9. (Upper image showing step 8 half-complete) Bring this edge up to meet the top edge, creating the creases shown as you flatten all the folds down.

10. (Lower image) The model should look like this. If it doesn't, Jabba will be very upset! Fold the left-pointed corner to the right along the center crease. Now repeat Steps 7 to 10 for the other side.

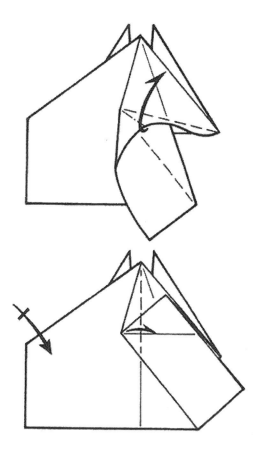

11. (Upper image) Fold the model in half.

12. (Lower image) Fold the wings and fins, and push in the fuselage to make a tail (used for atmospheric stability when descending to the desert planet Tatooine, for example).

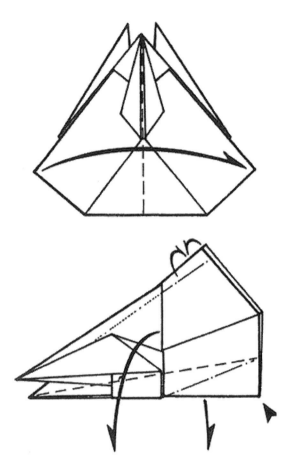

13. The completed Millennium Falcon MkII. Throw
horizontally with moderate force. Jabba will be
pleased!

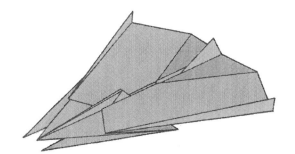

Stealth Wing

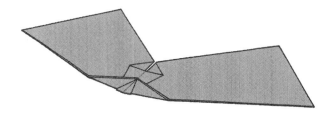

A little closer to Earth, some of our own reconnaissance and experimental craft can appear as something alien. Indeed, some of them can reach altitudes that virtually become space anyway. Their stealth designs make them difficult to see on radar, much as you would expect from an alien invader craft (just ask David Vincent, he has seen them!).

Regarding stealth, Lockheed bombers, for example, feature unusual air intakes designed to fragment radar waves, thus eliminating virtually all the energy though would otherwise have bounced back to tracking stations. Cool huh? And speaking of radar, this craft resembles a bat wing shape – and bats have their own radar too :)

1. (Upper image) Fold a sheet of Letter or A4 paper in half lengthwise.

2. (Lower image, larger view) Make all the creases shown.

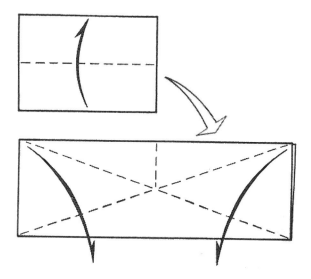

3. (Top image) Bring all the sides together to form a large rabbit-ear fold (noting the rabbit ear practice fold at the beginning of this book). Crease-fold right.

4. (Middle image) And then crease-fold left. Now tuck your finger inside the rabbit ear, opening out the paper and flattening the fold.

5. (Lower image) Almost there. Repeat for the other side.

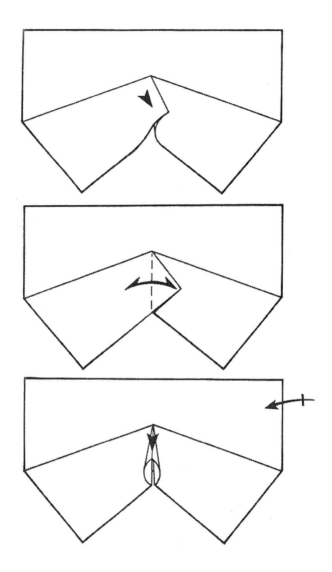

6. (Upper image) Open out the whole top section.

7. (Lower image) Fold the lower points inside as shown.

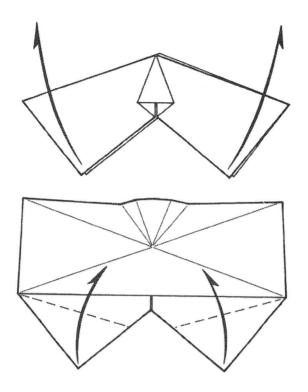

8. (Top image) Fold again.

9. (Middle image) Flatten the top section as it was in Step 6.

10. (Lower image) Fold the nose back by 1.5cm, and then fold the model across in half. Do not fold any part of the fuselage.

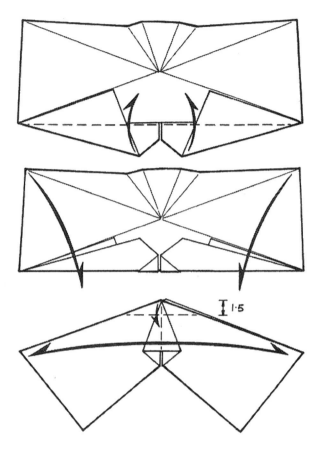

11. The completed stealth craft. Place your thumb underneath the center of the craft, forefinger over the top. With a forward motion of your arm, slowly let go of the craft. It will glide smoothly. Adjust the nose or tail section for more weight or lift respectively.

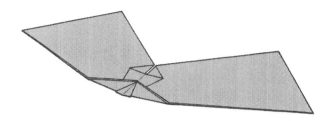

Since this is an experimental craft, try creating a solid fuselage 1cm high by folding the wings together and then folding down accordingly. Add a paperclip to the nose for weight and then you have a sturdier little craft you can throw with more force.

About the Author

Carmel Duryea Morris is a multi-talented designer and writer of some 35 books for children. These consist of 3D graphics art books such as *3D Magic Poster Book* (Dragons World) and *Flight Paths Through Time* (Simon & Schuster), fiction such as *Cod Almighty* (Scholastic) and Origami books such as *Fold Your Own Dinosaurs* and *Fold Your Own Creepy Crawlies* (Harper Collins). She began folding Origami models at the age of eight. Her *Advanced Paper Aircraft* Series and *The Best Paper Aircraft* series written under the pseudonym 'Campbell Morris' have sold hundreds of thousands of copies worldwide. She has appeared on *The Late Show* in LA and lectures at several universities on flight theory, teaching many young and old how to master paper aircraft building for fun, education, competitions and stress relief!

A software engineer, technical writer, sci-fi lover and ham radio geek girl, she also converted an old two-door sports coupe into an all-electric vehicle, using lithium phosphate batteries. She now drives happily around town without spending a dime on gas.

Made in the USA
Lexington, KY
17 April 2014